THANKS FOR THE MEMORIES

DAVID FISCHER AND DAVID ARETHA

SPORTS
PUBLISHING

Visit our website at www.sportspubbooks.com.

10 9 8 7 6 5 4 3 2 1

Library of Congress Cataloging-in-Publication Data is available on file.

Cover design by Tom Lau

Cover photo credit AP Photo/Elise Amendola

ISBN: 978-1-61321-965-2

Ebook ISBN: 978-1-61321-966-9

Printed in China

CONTENTS

Larger than Life

On November 18, 2015, his fortieth birthday, David Ortiz announced on ThePlayersTribune.com that he would retire after the 2016 season. "I wish I could play another forty years…." he said reflectively in the video. "We run out of time at some point. Life is based on different chapters, and I think I'm ready to experience the next one in my life."

While "Big Papi" explores new chapters, *these* chapters relive his storybook career. Ever since joining the Red Sox in 2003, David has been larger than life—from his monstrous home runs into the Boston sky, to his beaming smile and bear-sized hugs, to his enormous contributions to charity, to his heroic performances in so many postseason series. "Dang near every time, he comes through for us," teammate Coco Crisp once said.

Born and raised in Santo Domingo, Dominican Republic, David was blessed with the body and coordination to become a fine athlete. Everything else, he earned. Hardworking and intelligent, David studied his craft and honed his swing. He bashed his way to a professional contract with the Seattle Mariners at age seventeen and made it to the majors with Minnesota in 1997. But with the Twins, he struggled for six years—unsuccessfully—to become an everyday player. In January of 2002, his mother died. In December of that year, the Twins released him. The normally gregarious slugger grew somber.

A new father without a job, Ortiz fretted about his future. Would any team give him a second chance? Would he ever play in the majors again? In December 2002, Red Sox ace Pedro Martinez spotted David, his longtime Santo Domingo homie, in a local restaurant. David told him that the

Twins had let him go. Knowing the kind of teammate David could be, Pedro declared, "You're going to play for us!"

And did he ever.

Ortiz rocketed 31 home runs for Boston in 2003, but the best was yet to come. On October 18, 2004, at 1:22 a.m., David belted a 12th-inning homer against the Yankees in the ALCS that rivaled the excitement of Carlton Fisk's World Series clout in 1975. In the evening game that followed, also on October 18, Ortiz came through again, delivering a 14th-inning walk-off single. It turned out that the Red Sox needed a hero of David's physical and mental strength to eradicate the "Curse of the Bambino," which had plagued the franchise for 86 years.

The Red Sox stormed to the 2004 world title, and David became baseball's new Mr. October. His clutch postseason hitting resulted in World Series triumphs in 2007 and '13, the year he personified "Boston Strong" following the Boston Marathon bombings. In 2015, he surpassed 500 home runs and showed no letup in his production, topping 100 RBIs for the third straight year.

Through it all, Big Papi has embraced Red Sox Nation, both figuratively and literally. He has always taken time to hug, chat with, sign autographs for, and take pictures with Red Sox fans, young and old. David "carried a region through heartbreak," wrote Adam Kilgore of the *Washington Post*, "and made a city fall in love with him." All the while, he fell in love with the city.

Thanks for the memories, Big Papi, and keep swinging for the fences.

INNING 1

A PLAYER TO BE NAMED LATER

On August 29, 1996, Minnesota traded Dave Hollins to Seattle for a player to be named later. That player turned out to be David Arias, a slender, slick-fielding first baseman who had cracked .322-18-93 in the Class A Midwest League that season. In 1997, David Arias became David Ortiz and began a rocky six-year stint with the Minnesota Twins.

Like these kids in the Dominican Republic, David grew up in that nation's capital, Santo Domingo, playing baseball. David was the oldest of Enrique (a former pro baseball player) and Angela's four children. Easygoing and friendly, he starred in both basketball and baseball at Estudia Espallat High School, where he used his size, strength, and quickness to power to the hoop and jack balls over the right-field fence. All major league teams had a presence in this baseball-obsessed country, and the Seattle Mariners had their eye on Ortiz. They signed him on November 28, 1992, ten days after his seventeenth birthday.

"No matter where you're from or what you look like, if you play the game, you have something in common. You're a team. Everybody has a job to do. And that's all that really matters."
—David Ortiz

"He's been streaky. He'll get seven or eight hits in 10 at-bats, then he'll go seven or eight at-bats with nothing. But that's just a matter of maturity. The older he gets, the better he's going to be."
—Wisconsin Timber Rattlers manager Mike Goff on Ortiz in August 1996

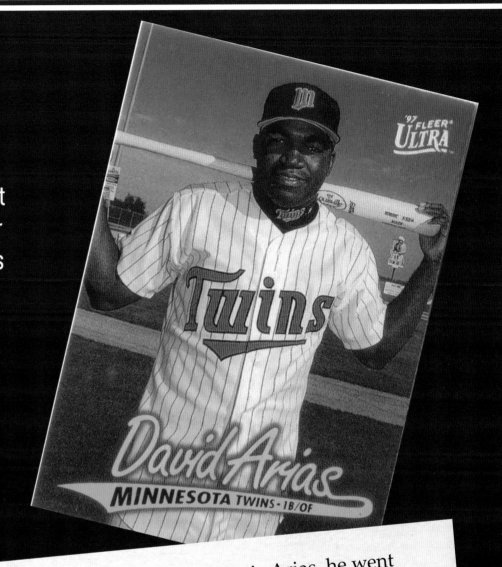

It's almost as if David Ortiz came out of nowhere. Born David Americo Ortiz Arias, he went by David Arias (his maternal last name) during his first three pro seasons—1994 to '96—all in the Seattle organization. Upon his trade to Minnesota in September 1996, David told the Twins that he wanted to be known as David Ortiz (his paternal surname)—but apparently the Fleer company had yet to get the memo. Ortiz tore it up in the minors in '97, smashing .317-31-124 while playing in Double-A and Triple-A for the first time.

Twins manager Tom Kelly (left) and coach Ron Gardenhire try to calm Ortiz after he was ejected on August 26, 2001, for arguing strike calls with the umpire. In his first five seasons with Minnesota, David's playing time was limited due to injuries, struggles against lefties, subpar defense at first base, questions about his intensity in the field, and the occasional outburst. From 1997 to 2001, he averaged just 66 games played, a .264 average, and nine homers per year. A tragic event after the 2001 season would change the course of his life and career.

TWINS
MAGAZINE

Season of Dedication

David Ortiz plays ball this season
with his late mother on his mind.

JUNE/JULY 2002 $4.00
www.twinsbaseball.com

"Everyone in the family, they all struggled when my mom died. My aunts. My uncles. My sister and my pop. I felt like I had to be the strong one, like I had to take care of everybody. That's what my mom would have done."
—David Ortiz

On New Year's Day, 2002, David's mother, Angela, died in a car crash. The grieving child responded by focusing harder than ever on baseball. After a slow start due in part to a knee injury, he broke through in the second half, smashing .297-15-42 in 65 games. In nine postseason contests, he batted .276.

The mascot of the Dominican Republic Aguilas congratulates Ortiz after he slammed a game-winning home run against the Puerto Rico Criollos in the Caribbean Series of Baseball in February 2003. For the coming season, David's salary was expected to jump from $950,000 to roughly $2 million because he was eligible for arbitration. Twins General Manager Terry Ryan viewed the slugger as too inconsistent and too expensive, and tried to trade him. He found no takers, and on December 16, 2002, the Twins released him. A month later, Ortiz found an MLB team that valued his services.

INNING 2

WELCOME TO RED SOX NATION

On January 22, 2003, a brutally cold day in Boston, few noticed that the Red Sox signed free agent David Ortiz (one year, $1.25 million). "A lot of people thought I was never going to be more than what I was at the time," David said, "a part-time designated hitter who had some power but wasn't productive enough to play every day." He would soon prove them all so wrong.

In December 2002, Ortiz sat glumly in a Santo Domingo restaurant. All of a sudden, his old buddy Pedro Martinez (right), Boston's pitching ace, walked in. David told him he just got released by the Twins. Ortiz recalled the story on ThePlayersTribune.com.

"Oh my God. This is amazing," Martinez said.

"What the hell are you talking about, bro? I just had a kid. I don't know what I'm gonna do."

Pedro pulled out his cell phone and left the restaurant. A couple minutes later he returned. He told David that he just got off the phone with Boston GM Theo Epstein.

"You're going to play for us!" Martinez said. "Well, actually, I just got Epstein's voice mail. But I told him that you're a special player and he's gotta sign you. We need you, man. We need you!"

"For real?"

"For real, homie."

Batting just .188 on April 27, 2003, David socked a 14th-inning homer at Anaheim that night—his first big fly as a Red Sox—to begin his ascension. Batting primarily fifth in the order behind masher Manny Ramirez, Ortiz set personal highs across the board that year (.288-31-101). Here he celebrates a walk-off homer against Baltimore on September 23—a key blow for a Boston team (95-67) that would win the wild-card spot by just two games over Seattle.

David wielded magic with this "Big Stick" bat and black and red batting gloves. Red sweat bands (with the number 34 on them) and a right elbow protector were also part of his repertoire.

MOST 30-HOMER SEASONS IN RED SOX HISTORY	
David Ortiz	9
Ted Williams	8
Manny Ramirez	6
Jimmie Foxx	5
Jim Rice	4
Mo Vaughn	4

MOST 100-RBI SEASONS IN RED SOX HISTORY	
David Ortiz	9
Ted Williams	9
Jim Rice	8
Bobby Doerr	6
Jimmie Foxx	6
Manny Ramirez	6

David's legendary postseason heroics began in 2003. At sun-splashed Fenway Park in Game 4 of the ALDS, he smashed a two-run double off the 380 sign in right for the final runs of a 5–4 win over Oakland. Here, in Game 6 of the ALCS against the Yankees, he strokes a two-run single in the third inning off Andy Pettitte, sparking a 9–6 Boston win. The next day, he homered in the eighth to give the Sox a *seemingly* comfortable 5–2 lead.

David slumps against the couch of the visitors' clubhouse after an agonizing loss in Game 7 of the 2003 ALCS. Manager Grady Little left Pedro Martinez in too long—according to critics—and New York scored three in the bottom of the eighth to tie the game at 5–5. Ortiz doubled in the 10th, but no one scored until Yankees third baseman Aaron Boone homered in the bottom of the 11th. The Curse of the Bambino had struck again.

INNING 3

THE ROAR OF '04

Following a 19-8 loss to the Yankees, the Red Sox trailed in the 2004 ALCS three games to none. All seemed hopeless...until a hero emerged. David blasted a 12th-inning walk-off homer in Game 4 and a game-ending 14th-inning single the next night. "He didn't do it again, did he?" asked broadcaster Tim McCarver. "Yes, he did!" Boston's 86-year title drought was about to end.

Ortiz points to the heavens and Ben Davis stares at the ground after Big Papi's eighth-inning solo homer gave Boston a 6–5 lead over the White Sox on August 22, 2004. After his breakthrough year in 2003, David took his hitting to an even higher level in '04, setting personal bests in batting, homers, and RBIs (.301-41-139) as well as doubles (47) and walks (75). He finished fourth in AL MVP voting and won the Silver Slugger Award.

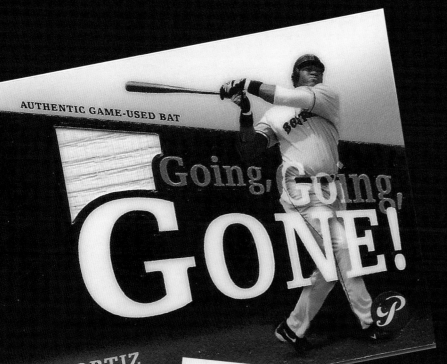

AUTHENTIC GAME-USED BAT

Going, Going, GONE!

DAVID ORTIZ
BOSTON RED SOX®

"There are few sweeter sights for the Boston Red Sox than Ortiz walking to the plate with a black bat in his hands and a white ball on his radar."
—Jack Curry, *New York Times*

This 2004 Topps Pristine card includes real lumber from an Ortiz bat. That year, 41 of his fly balls went, went, and left, as he finished second in the league in bombs behind teammate Manny Ramirez (43). While David swatted his iconic home runs at Fenway Park throughout his career, he launched most of his big flys on the road, including 24 of the 41 in '04. Fenway requires a 380-foot poke to right field, unless you pull it down the line.

In 2004, Ortiz furthered his legend by belting a home run in his very first All-Star Game. Here, in the sixth inning, he and Florida Marlins pitcher Carl Pavano watch the towering shot sail into the upper deck in right-center field at Minute Maid Park in Houston. David walked, homered, and walked after entering the game in the fourth inning.

"Yeah, I did say something stupid like that."
—David Ortiz, when asked to confirm that he had predicted in the ninth inning that he would win the game

David's wide-eyed teammates and fans watch his towering fly ball sail over the Green Monster to clinch the 2004 ALDS. Boston had taken the first two games in Anaheim, 9–3 and 8–3. Game 3 went to the bottom of the 10th tied at 6–6 before Ortiz ended it with this two-out, two-run shot. In 16 plate appearances in the series, Big Papi tallied a homer, two doubles, three singles, and five walks for a .688 OBP.

David rounds first after belting a walk-off homer in Game 4 of the 2004 ALCS. Down three games to none to New York, the Red Sox tied this game in the ninth, 4–4, when Bill Mueller drove in pinch runner Dave Roberts (who had stolen second base) with a single off Mariano Rivera. With Manny Ramirez on base in the 12th, Ortiz rainbowed a homer into the right field seats, triggering bedlam at 1:22 a.m. "This is a team that never gives up," David said amid the postgame delirium.

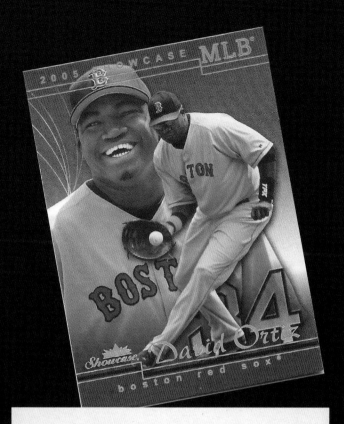

David's 2005 trading card, a season when he hit two walk-off homers.

"Ortiz was taking a trendy baseball term—the 'walk-off'—and making it a subheading on his résumé."
—Tony Massarotti, author of *Big Papi: My Story of Big Dreams and Big Hits*

BIG PAPI'S WALK-OFF HOMERS FOR BOSTON

Date	Opp.	Inn.	Men On	Final	Location
9/23/03	BAL	10th	0	6–5	Left
4/11/04	TOR	12th	1	6–4	Left
10/8/04	ANA	10th	1	8–6	Left*
10/17/04	NYY	12th	1	6–4	Right+
6/2/05	BAL	9th	2	6–4	Center
9/6/05	LAA	9th	0	3–2	Right
6/11/06	TEX	9th	2	5–4	Right
6/24/06	PHI	10th	1	5–3	Center
7/31/06	CLE	9th	2	9–8	Center
9/12/07	TAM	9th	1	5–4	Right
8/26/09	CWS	9th	0	3–2	Right
6/6/13	TEX	9th	2	6–3	Right

*Series-clinching homer in Game 3 of ALDS

+Game 4 of ALCS

After beginning October 18 with an epic homer, David ends it with a walk-off single. Boston seemed doomed in the eighth inning of Game 5 of the ALCS, trailing 4–2, but an Ortiz homer and a Jason Varitek sac fly tied the score at 4–4. With two outs and runners on first and second in the 14th, Big Papi fouled off *eight* two-strike pitches (one nearly missed the Pesky Pole in right) before blooping a winning single to center. The Sox were still alive.

THE WALK-OFFS: PITCH BY PITCH

2004 ALDS, Game 3

Situation: The Red Sox lead the series 2–0 and are trying to clinch it with a win at Fenway Park. The score is 6–6 in the bottom of the 10th. Against lefty Jarrod Washburn, Ortiz bats with two outs and Pokey Reese on first.

Pitch 1: Ortiz lofts a fly ball over the Green Monster in left for a two-run walk-off homer.

2004 ALCS, Game 4

Situation: The Yankees lead the series 3–0 and are trying to clinch at Fenway. The Red Sox, after tying the game with a run in the ninth, bat in the bottom of the 12th with the score still 4–4. Manny Ramirez leads off with a single, and Ortiz steps to the plate against right-hander Paul Quantrill.

Pitch 1: Breaking ball low; 1–0.

Pitch 2: Called strike on the inside corner, 1–1.

Pitch 3: Ball in the dirt; 2–1.

Pitch 4: Ortiz rockets an inside pitch into the Red Sox bullpen in right, giving Boston a 6–4 victory at 1:22 a.m.

2004 ALCS, Game 5

Situation: After Boston tied the game 4–4 in the eighth (thanks in part to an Ortiz homer), the score remains 4–4 in the bottom of the 14th. Ortiz bats with two outs, Manny Ramirez on first, and Johnny Damon on second. Esteban Loaiza, who walked both of those batters, now faces Big Papi.

Pitch 1: Ortiz swings and misses on an outside pitch; 0–1.

Pitch 2: Ball high and away; 1–1.

Pitch 3: Fouled back; 1–2.

Pitch 4: Fouled back; 1–2.

Pitch 5: Fouled deep down the right-field line; 1–2.

Pitch 6: Ball way outside; 2–2.

Pitch 7: Fouled back on a massive cut; 2–2.

Pitch 8: Fouled back; 2–2.

Pitch 9: Fouled into the left-field stands; 2–2.

Pitch 10: Ortiz bloops a single into center field, scoring Damon with the winning run.

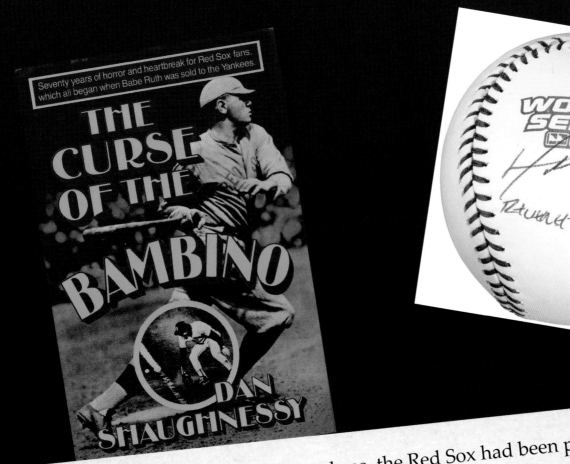

Seventy years of horror and heartbreak for Red Sox fans, which all began when Babe Ruth was sold to the Yankees.

THE CURSE OF THE BAMBINO

DAN SHAUGHNESSY

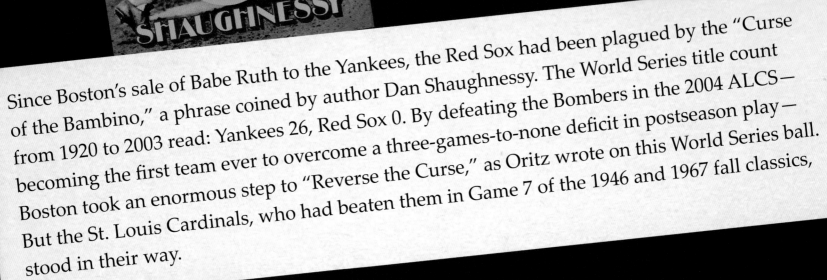

Since Boston's sale of Babe Ruth to the Yankees, the Red Sox had been plagued by the "Curse of the Bambino," a phrase coined by author Dan Shaughnessy. The World Series title count from 1920 to 2003 read: Yankees 26, Red Sox 0. By defeating the Bombers in the 2004 ALCS—becoming the first team ever to overcome a three-games-to-none deficit in postseason play—Boston took an enormous step to "Reverse the Curse," as Oritz wrote on this World Series ball. But the St. Louis Cardinals, who had beaten them in Game 7 of the 1946 and 1967 fall classics, stood in their way.

Johnny Damon and Orlando Cabrera revere "Big Papi" after he plated them with a three-run homer in the first inning of Game 1 of the 2004 World Series. Fenway Park erupted as David's rocket to right shot past the good side of the foul pole. "Ortiz has done it again!" declared Fox announcer Joe Buck. St. Louis tied the game at 9–9, but a Mark Bellhorn two-run homer in the eighth won it for Boston, 11–9.

Pedro Martinez, Curt Schilling, and Ortiz celebrate a well-earned sweep of St. Louis in the World Series. Pedro pitched seven shutout innings in a 4–1 Game 3 victory. Schilling, who had won Game 6 of the ALCS on a surgically repaired and bleeding ankle (his famous *red sock*), earned the W in Game 3 against the Cardinals. Oritz batted .400 with five homers and 19 RBIs (tying an MLB record) in the postseason.

A caravan transports the world champion Red Sox through the streets of Boston on Saturday, October 30, 2004, while one woman touts a sign that reads, "MARRY ME ORTIZ." The Associated Press reported: "On a raw autumn day with spitting rain, an estimated 3.2 million people packed the 7-mile parade route, hanging from windows, standing on rooftops, and holding aloft signs bearing words of thanks, marriage proposals, and expressions of wonder at what the team had—finally—accomplished." This victory parade remains the largest public gathering in American history.

David hoists the World Series trophy during the victory parade. Celebrating the championship they had coveted all their lives, fans were giddy with excitement. Two twenty-three-year-old men from Worcester wore self-inflating sumo wrestler outfits to represent Ortiz and Manny Ramirez. Santa Lopez, thirty-seven, played a guira, a musical instrument from her native Dominican Republic. David expressed his approval by pointing at her with both index fingers—a thrill she would never forget. "I feel crazy!" she exclaimed.

INNING 4

MASTER BLASTER

In 2005–06, Ortiz blasted 101 home runs, becoming the first Red Sox slugger ever to reach triple digits over a two-year span. Big Papi became the most feared hitter in the league and led the AL in RBIs both seasons. David, who powered Boston to the playoffs in 2005, broke the team's season home run record the following year. These two campaigns marked the physical peak of his illustrious career.

Edgar Renteria hugs Ortiz after the big hero's second homer of the game on September 20, 2005. David led the AL in RBIs (148) that year while finishing second in homers (47) and walks (102) and third in runs (119), total bases (363), and OPS (1.001). Twenty of his big flys tied the score or put the Red Sox ahead. Ortiz was named Player of the Month for September/October after belting .321-11-30 and knocking a walk-off homer against the Angels and a game-ending single versus the Blue Jays.

The 2004 Red Sox World Series
championship ring includes the inscription
"GREATEST COMEBACK IN HISTORY."

On a crisp, sun-splashed Opening Day in 2005, Ortiz proudly displays the ring he earned for winning the previous year's World Series. Yankees players watched in envy, then suffered a humiliating 8-1 defeat. Later that day, actor Ben Affleck took a jab at the bling-loving DH, saying that "Ortiz's ring is only his fourth-largest piece of jewelry."

> "I love Manny. He's a great guy and a great player, but after the game was over, Manny's life was different. Half an hour after the game was over, I didn't know about Manny until 2:30 the next day."
> —David Ortiz

The Sox boasted a potent lineup in 2005. That season, Ortiz (usually the three-hole hitter) and Manny Ramirez (cleanup) formed one of the greatest slugging duos of all time. By crushing .292-45-144, Ramirez finished .008-2-4 behind Big Papi. They powered an offense that led the majors in runs (910) and twice massacred the Yankees 17–1. Despite a rotation whose top five starters had ERAs in the 4.00s, the Sox bashed their way to a 95–67 record and a wild-card berth. The Yankees finished with an identical record but won the AL East Division due to a better fate in head-to-head matchups (10–9).

BOSTON
August 24, 2005

		8
1	DAMON (L)	6
2	RENTERIA	DH
3	ORTIZ (L)	7
4	RAMIREZ	9
5	NIXON (L)	2
6	VARITEK (S)	3
7	MILLAR	5
8	MUELLER (S)	4
9	GRAFFANINO	SP
P	CLEMENT	

LH	EXTRAS	RH
CORA		MIRABELLI
PETAGINE		KAPLER
OLERUD		

LH	PITCHERS	RH
MYERS		GONZALEZ
REMLINGER		BRADFORD
		TIMLIN
		PAPELBON

Ortiz slides in safely with a third-inning double in Game 2 of the 2005 ALDS. While this two-bagger helped Boston go up 4–0, a three-run homer by Tadahito Iguchi (pictured) in the fifth keyed a 5–4 White Sox victory. Chicago also won Games 1 (14–2) and 3 (5–3) to complete the sweep, with David hitting .333 with one homer in the series. One season after the Red Sox broke their 86-year curse, the Chicago White Sox won the World Series that year for their first title in 88 years.

During Game 4 of the 2005 World Series in Houston, Henry Aaron presents Ortiz and Atlanta's Andruw Jones with Hank Aaron Awards, presented yearly to the best overall hitter in each league. During his peak years of 2004 through '07, David won a Silver Slugger Award each year (the only player to win four straight as a DH) and finished fourth, second, third, and fourth in AL MVP Award voting. His 47 homers and 148 RBIs in '05 were numbers "Hammerin' Hank" never achieved.

"[Ortiz] is the most popular back home right now. With his personality and the patriotism he has shown in playing here, he is the idol of an entire country. And he has earned it. He's a legit guy. There's no bluffing his way through this. He is what you see."
—Manny Acta, Dominican Republic manager, 2006 World Baseball Classic

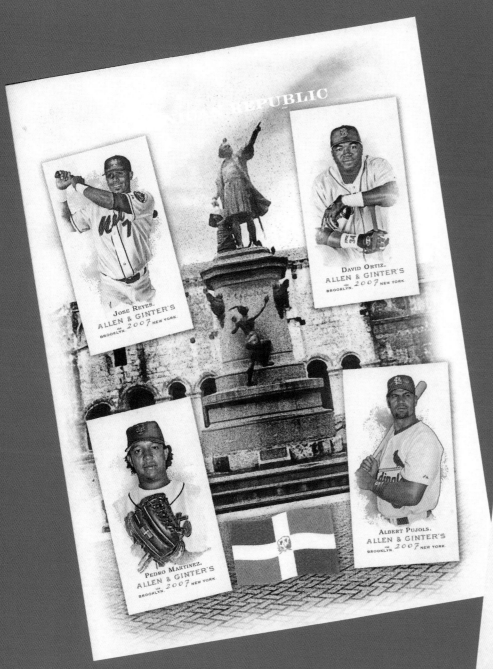

In 2006, Manny Ramirez opted not to participate in the inaugural World Baseball Classic, which disappointed his countrymen in the Dominican Republic. But Ortiz proudly represented his nation and even belted three home runs in the tournament, leading the Dominican Republic to the semifinals. Here he's pictured on a 2007 Topps collage with three other Dominican stars: Jose Reyes and Pedro Martinez, then of the Mets, and Albert Pujols, who was with the Cardinals.

Yankees catcher Jorge Posada watches David's fly ball disappear into the Yankee Stadium crowd on May 10, 2006. Big Papi led the AL with 54 home runs that year while tying the league record for road homers with 32, set by Babe Ruth in 1927. Ortiz became the first player to lead his circuit in homers, RBIs (137), and walks (119) since Mike Schmidt in 1981. He also finished second in the AL in slugging (.636) and third in runs (115).

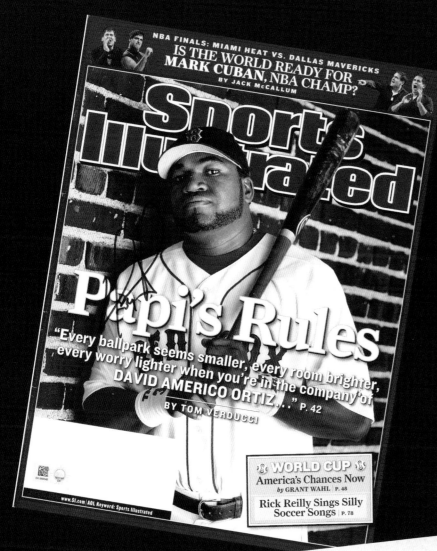

"In girth and mirth Ortiz evokes Babe Ruth, Santa Claus and your favorite stuffed animal from childhood."
—*Sports Illustrated* writer Tom Verducci

Ortiz graces a *Sports Illustrated* cover dated June 19, 2006. Writer Tom Verducci's assessment of David—"Every ballpark seems smaller, every room brighter, every worry lighter when you're in the company of David Americo Ortiz"—was so spot-on that the words opened the story and appeared on the cover.

Teammates mob Big Papi after his three-run homer in the bottom of the ninth defeated Cleveland 9–8 on July 31, 2006, keeping Boston a game up on the Yankees in the AL East. Ortiz belted three walk-off homers that season, one short of the MLB record, and socked them all within a 51-day span. He victimized Texas with a three-run shot in the ninth inning on June 11 and Philadelphia with a 10th-inning homer on June 24. Oh, and he also drilled walk-off singles on June 26 and July 29.

On September 21, 2006, Ortiz slugged his 51st homer of the year, breaking Jimmie Foxx's Red Sox record. In a ceremony five days later, Jimmie's daughter, Nanci Foxx Cannaday (far left), and Linda Ruth Tosetti, a granddaughter of Babe Ruth, honored David's mighty achievement. David's wife, Tiffany, and their children, Alexandra and D'Angelo, celebrated the historic feat.

DAVID ORTIZ'S CAREER STATISTICS

Year	Tm	G	AB	R	H	2B	3B	HR	RBI	SB	BB	BA	OBP	SLG	OPS	TB	HBP
1997	MIN	15	49	10	16	3	0	1	6	0	2	.327	.353	.449	.802	22	0
1998	MIN	86	278	47	77	20	0	9	46	1	39	.277	.371	.446	.817	124	5
1999	MIN	10	20	1	0	0	0	0	0	0	5	.000	.200	.000	.200	0	0
2000	MIN	130	415	59	117	36	1	10	63	1	57	.282	.364	.446	.810	185	0
2001	MIN	89	303	46	71	17	1	18	48	1	40	.234	.324	.475	.799	144	1
2002	MIN	125	412	52	112	32	1	20	75	1	43	.272	.339	.500	.839	206	3
2003	BOS	128	448	79	129	39	2	31	101	0	58	.288	.369	.592	.961	265	1
2004*	BOS	150	582	94	175	47	3	41	139	0	75	.301	.380	.603	.983	351	4
2005*	BOS	159	601	119	180	40	1	47	**148**	1	102	.300	.397	.604	1.001	363	1
2006*	BOS	151	558	115	160	29	2	**54**	**137**	1	**119**	.287	.413	.636	1.049	**355**	4
2007*	BOS	149	549	116	182	52	1	35	117	3	**111**	.332	**.445**	.621	1.066	341	4
2008*	BOS	109	416	74	110	30	1	23	89	1	70	.264	.369	.507	.877	211	1
2009	BOS	150	541	77	129	35	1	28	99	0	74	.238	.332	.462	.794	250	5
2010*	BOS	145	518	86	140	36	1	32	102	0	82	.270	.370	.529	.899	274	2
2011*	BOS	146	525	84	162	40	1	29	96	1	78	.309	.398	.554	.953	291	1
2012*	BOS	90	324	65	103	26	0	23	60	0	56	.318	.415	.611	1.026	198	0
2013*	BOS	137	518	84	160	38	2	30	103	4	76	.309	.395	.564	.959	292	1
2014	BOS	142	518	59	136	27	0	35	104	0	75	.263	.355	.517	.873	268	3
2015	BOS	146	528	73	144	37	0	37	108	0	77	.273	.360	.553	.913	292	0

*All-Star season

Bold: led league

INNING 5

BASEBALL HEAVEN IN '07

The Red Sox entered 2007 facing questions about their lineup, starting staff, and bullpen. David helped provide the answers, batting a career-high .332 while sacrificing little of his prodigious power. The Angels couldn't keep him off base in the ALDS, and he helped carry Boston to their second World Series title in four years.

During David's tenure in Boston, the Red Sox were a team that overcame, from "Reverse the Curse" in 2004 to "Boston Strong" in '13. In 2007, the Sox fielded two key contributors who had overcome cancer. Third baseman Mike Lowell (right), who was diagnosed with testicular cancer in 1999, joined the Red Sox in 2006 and ripped .324-21-120 on an '07 Sox team that needed his lumber. In August 2006, rookie pitcher Jon Lester (left) learned he had a treatable form of lymphoma. He came back to go 4–0 in 11 starts in '07. Both men would form charitable organizations to help others battle cancer.

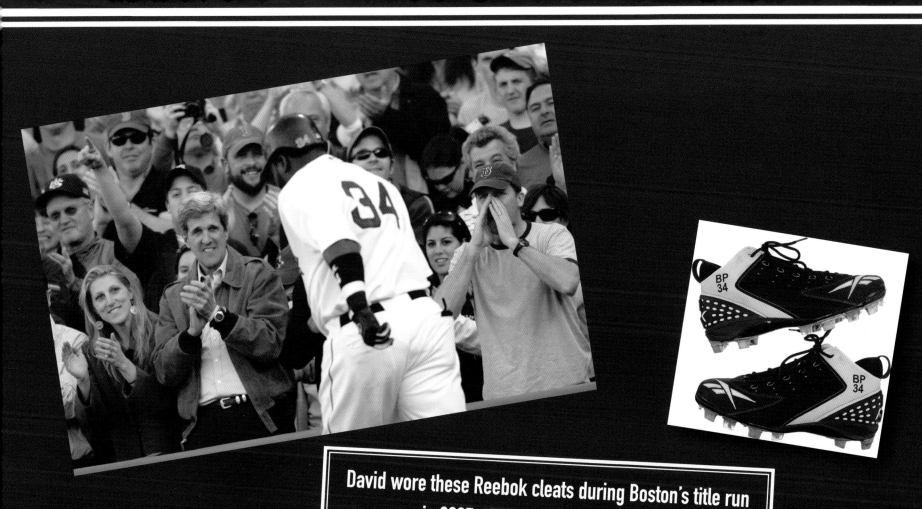

David wore these Reebok cleats during Boston's title run in 2007. "BP" stands for "Big Papi."

US Senator John Kerry (D-MA), his daughter Vanessa, and everyone else in Fenway laud Ortiz after his home run against the Yankees on April 21, 2007. Big Papi drove in 22 runs in 24 games in April to push the Sox to a 16–8 record and an AL East lead that they would never relinquish. David hit .314-14-52 in the first half, and was voted a starter for the All-Star Game.

Mickey Mantle and Ortiz, featured on this 2007 Topps Heritage card, each boasted a career high of 54 home runs.

AL Players with 500 Homers, 500 Doubles, 1,500 RBIs, 1,000 walks
Babe Ruth
Ted Williams
Carl Yastrzemski
Rafael Palmeiro
Alex Rodriguez
David Ortiz

MLB Players with 3 World Series Titles and 500 Home Runs
Babe Ruth
Mickey Mantle
Reggie Jackson
David Ortiz

"Never in a million years did I think I would tie a record that would put me right there next to Babe Ruth."
—David Ortiz

Ortiz and Angels catcher Jeff Mathis speculate on the distance of his grand slam on August 18, 2007. After David's 54-bomb season in 2006, pitchers tried to keep balls out of his wheelhouse in '07. He responded by using the whole field more (career highs in average, .332, and doubles, 52) and laying off pitches (AL best in walks, 111, and in OBP, .445). He also belted 35 homers, scored 116 runs, and drove in 117. Big Papi, who batted .365 at home, stroked .352-21-65 in 68 second-half games.

David sprays champagne after the Red Sox clinched the AL East title on September 28, 2007—their first division crown in 12 years. Boston defeated Minnesota 5–2 and then celebrated 77 minutes later when the Yankees were eliminated by Baltimore. Big Papi's AL Player of the Month performance in September (.396-9-27) helped the Sox fend off the charging Yankees by two games in the AL East. Like Carl Yastrzemski in 1967, Ortiz raged at season's end, going 10-for-12 from September 26–28 and reaching base 11 straight times.

"I do nothing but fight back. That's me."
—David Ortiz, after the division-clinching victory

Ortiz rockets a home run over Angels pitcher Jared Weaver's head in the fourth inning of Game 4 of the 2007 AL Division Series. Manny Ramirez followed with a big fly to give the Red Sox a 2–0 lead, and they romped 9–1 to clinch the series. After hitting .552 with a .639 OBP over his final eight regular-season games, David went 5-for-7 (.717) with six walks (.846 OBP) in the ALDS. Ramirez rapped .375-2-4. "They're the best combo I've ever seen," said Boston reliever Eric Gagne. "They're clutch. They thrive on pressure, and that's what it's all about."

David congratulates Manny Ramirez after the latter's home run in Game 2 of the 2007 ALCS. Reminiscent of the 2004 Championship Series against the Yankees, Boston roared back from a three-games-to-one deficit to defeat Cleveland in the 2007 ALCS. The Indians won Game 2 13-6 in 11 innings and then took the next two games at Jacobs Field. The Sox responded with 7–1, 12–2, and 11–2 rampages. Ramirez and Mike Lowell drove in a combined 18 runs, while Ortiz contributed a .292 average, six walks, and seven runs.

A sweep of Arizona in the 2007 NLCS gave Colorado 21 victories in its previous 22 games, but an eight-day wait to start the World Series cooled the Rockies. The Red Sox, meanwhile, continued their torrid hitting in Game 1, romping 13–1 at Fenway as Ortiz contributed two RBI doubles and a single. Here he bumps with Dustin Pedroia after the feisty second baseman (and AL Rookie of the Year) led off the first inning with a home run.

Shortstop Julio Lugo looks to join catcher Jason Varitek and pitcher Jonathon Papelbon after the closer fanned Seth Smith to end Game 4, giving Boston a World Series sweep. Ortiz put the Red Sox ahead to stay with an RBI single in the first inning. They moved ahead 3–0 and then 4–1 until Colorado made it close with a two-run homer in the eighth, but Papelbon retired the Rockies 1-2-3 in the ninth. The pitcher took the title-clinching ball home, where his dog tore it to shreds. As for Boston's top dog, Ortiz, he batted .333-0-4 in the series.

"This is about the whole team, not all about one or two players. This is the Red Sox right here. I told everybody, you've got to feel proud of wearing this name on your chest. You're good at something."
—David Ortiz, after the title-clinching victory

By pressing the brim of this bobblehead's cap, Big Papi would confirm that, yes, the Red Sox did indeed win their second World Series title in 2007.

"When I came here in 2003, it seemed like it was impossible to win a World Series. And now this is my second. It's unbelievable!"
—David Ortiz

The Boston Globe trumpets the news of the World Series sweep. On Monday, October 30, the Globe reported that large throngs of fans greeted the players at Boston's Logan Airport and then along Yawkey Way: "While they waited for the buses to arrive [at Fenway Park], they chanted 'Let's Go Red Sox,' sang 'Sweet Caroline,' and bounced around beach balls as if it were the bleachers."

David added a second World Series ring to his abundant jewelry collection.

Fans in Boston's Copley Square honor their heroes during the World Series victory parade on Tuesday, October 30, 2007. Sox players and their families boarded twenty World War II–era duck boats outside Fenway Park and began a journey through the city. During the two-hour parade, reliever Jonathan Papelbon donned a kilt and danced a jig while Manny Ramirez proclaimed to the city, "There's a party at my house tonight!" Responding to a fan who asked when the Red Sox would clinch a World Series at home, Ortiz responded, "Dude, it doesn't matter where you win it, as long as you win it."

INNING 6

SHARING THE LOVE

With a heart as big as his swing, David has touched people in profound ways. He oversees the David Ortiz Children's Fund, which helps ailing children in New England and the Dominican Republic, and has contributed to numerous other charitable causes—the Jimmy Fund, Make-a-Wish, and the Papi Cares ticket program, to name a few. All the while, he elevates moods with his beaming smile, bear hugs, and infectious sense of humor.

Passion runs deep among Red Sox Nation, and David reflects that sentiment most of all. After finishing in last place in 2012, the Sox used these words on the cover of their 2013 season schedule. It didn't take long for the faith to be restored.

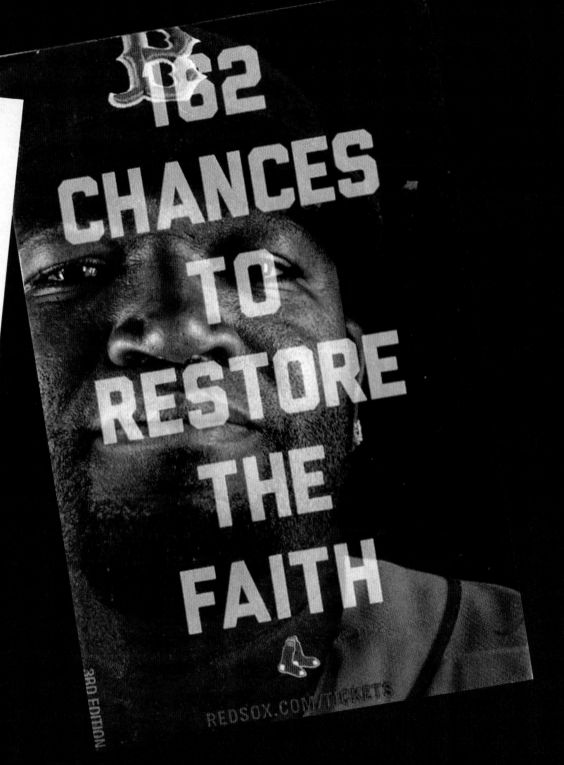

B 162 CHANCES TO RESTORE THE FAITH

3RD EDITION

REDSOX.COM/TICKETS

David embraces Amber DaRosa, a six-year-old girl with acute lymphocytic leukemia, at Fenway Park in 2004. This picture was used on billboards and in advertisements to promote the Jimmy Fund and became a powerful symbol of the team's commitment to help pediatric cancer patients. Today, Amber is in complete remission.

"I'm telling you, a bad day at the field is not even close to what they go through. A bad day on the field, you can replace it the following day. Sick people, a sick kid, there is no way to replace that until somebody makes a move to help the children out."
—David Ortiz

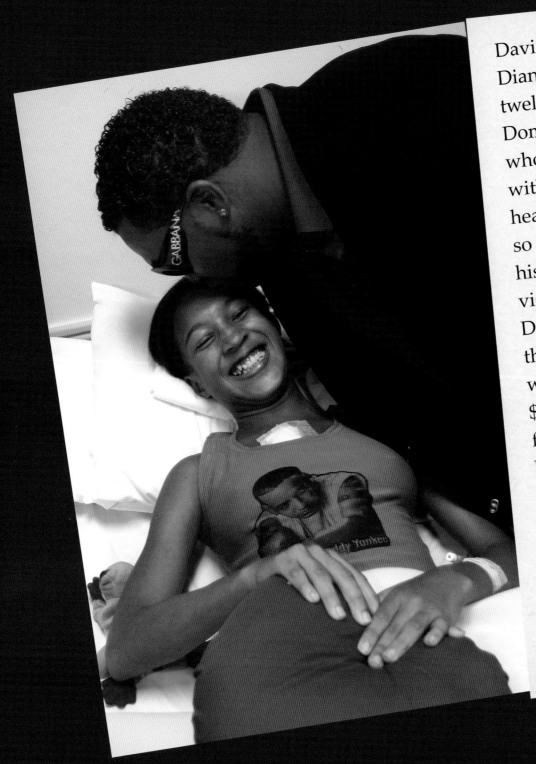

David kisses Diana Reyes, a twelve-year-old Dominican girl who was born with a hole in her heart. Ortiz was so moved during his December 2006 visit to this Santo Domingo hospital that he returned with a check for $200,000—a gift from him and the Boston Red Sox Foundation. The donation was enough to start the first pediatric cardiovascular unit in the Dominican Republic.

In 2015, Big Papi hosted the eighth annual David Ortiz Celebrity Golf Classic at the Sanctuary Capa Cana resort in the Dominican Republic. All told, David's duffers have raised more than $1 million to help disadvantaged youth in New England and the Dominican Republic receive needed health care. Bobby Orr, Bill Russell, Alex Rodriguez, and Mariano Rivera are among the many superstars who have teed up at the Ortiz Classic.

When Ortiz went down to Triple-A Pawtucket for a rehab assignment in July 2008, young Rhode Islanders fished for his autograph at McCoy Stadium. During this game against Toledo on July 17, 11,460 fans packed the 10,031-seat ballpark and chanted "Pa-pi! Pa-pi!" — inspiring him to swat a home run in the fourth inning. "That's exactly what happens at Fenway," Ortiz said after the game. "When they start chanting your name, it pumps you up and puts you in the mood."

David and Dustin Pedroia, two big-hearted heroes, have been though the wars together, winning world titles in 2007 and 2013. "When I go back to my country, I get questions about that guy every day," Ortiz told NESN. "I tell them the truth: he's a trouper and he's a great teammate.... That guy, he's like my brother. We're family." Pedroia praised the big fella for his work ethic and intelligence, saying he has taught many others how to approach hitters.

"David, he's a freak. He's like a superhero. He's like that in real life, too, and I think that's why everything about him is so endearing, because he is a genuine person and people here love him, and there's a reason why."
—Former Red Sox pitcher Josh Beckett

As much as he loves Dustin Pedroia, Ortiz isn't above humiliating the pint-sized second sacker. Here, on St. Patrick's Day, 2009, the legendary prankster tapes No. 15—Pedroia's number—to the back of a tiny leprechaun. The Red Sox list Dustin's height at 5-foot-9, but he admits that the team is an inch too generous.

David jokes with former Red Sox teammate Manny Ramirez (middle) and Kevin Millar on May 28, 2014. Though dead serious on the field, Big Papi loves to laugh and joke around. While with the Twins, Ortiz pranked his teammates by cutting off the toe area of their socks, and he once put Corey Koskie's street clothes in a freezer until they were frozen stiff. After Koskie retaliated by smearing peanut butter in David's underwear, Ortiz got him back with Icy Hot in Corey's undies. With the Red Sox, Big Papi has slammed shaving cream pies into the faces of teammates, and once he poured a pitcher of milk on outfielder Coco Crisp's head during a photo shoot.

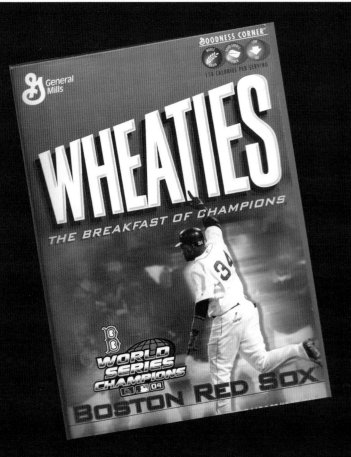

After his heroics in the 2004 postseason, David was feted on license plates and Wheaties boxes. In New England households, this Oritz toy socks fellow action-figure superheroes into oblivion.

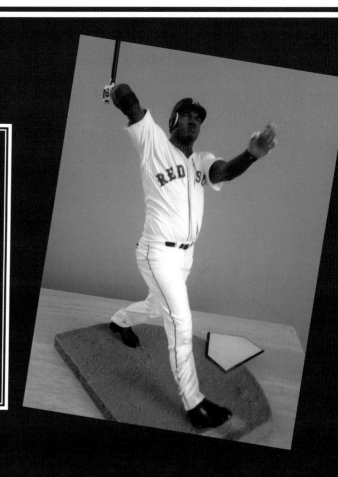

INNING 7

THE HEART OF THE ORDER

Despite the Red Sox' inability to bring another World Series trophy to Boston from 2008 to 2012, David's unrivaled reputation as the team's indomitable leader was cemented by his knack for the clutch hit—and for his intangible ability to create strong bonds by uniting people of all ages and different backgrounds.

David showed off the World Series trophy at the White House in Washington, D.C., on February 27, 2008, after a ceremony where President George W. Bush honored the 2007 champions. "The Mighty Red Sox Nation has stormed the South Lawn," said President Bush, the former owner of the Texas Rangers. "I love the fact that you've got some of the game's biggest stars [here]. I mean, Big Papi, the guy lights up the screen. He brings a great personality."

The defending world champion Red Sox got off to a flying start in 2008, and so did David. At the end of May, he was leading the team with 13 home runs and 43 RBIs. But in June, an awkward swing resulted in a serious left wrist injury, which cost David 53 missed games.

This is one of many Big Papi bobbleheads produced over the years—and is certainly the coolest.

While recuperating from injury, David became a United States citizen at the John F. Kennedy Library in Boston on June 11, 2008. During the 40-minute naturalization ceremony, David and 226 other immigrants from 57 countries took the oath of citizenship and then recited the Pledge of Allegiance. "My whole family, my kids and everyone, have been born here," Ortiz said. "America is a great country. I'm proud to be here, and now proud to be a part of it."

David returned from injury with a bang in 2008, here launching the first of two three-run home runs in the first inning of a wild 19-17 win over the Texas Rangers at Fenway on August 12. The occasion was historic. Besides David, only three other players in Red Sox history have belted two homers in the same inning: Nomar Garciaparra in 2002, Ellis Burks in 1990, and Bill Regan in 1928. And only two other Red Sox players have driven in six runs in one inning: Carlos Quintana in 1991 and Tom McBride in 1945.

"For every home run, clutch hit, or World Series trophy, there was David Ortiz, just as often, out of sight in the tunnel behind the Red Sox dugout, meeting a child before the game. His hug, his smile, and his relentless encouragement have comforted and inspired so many children. They understand the broader dimension that merits our calling him a hero."
—Red Sox Chairman Tom Werner

Big Papi tosses batting practice to his son, D'Angelo, at home plate before a game at Fenway Park, on August 31, 2008. That year UNICEF honored David with its Children's Champion Award in recognition of his work in children's health care. As for the adorable D'Angelo, he went on to become a switch-hitter—as well as a great interview. "Let me tell you something," he told Boston.com at age six. "My dad is *not* becoming a switch-hitter. He tries to hit righty but—look—he doesn't."

David soaked up the exhilaration while celebrating in the Fenway clubhouse on September 23 after Boston clinched its wild-card spot for the 2008 postseason. In the AL Division Series, the Red Sox easily dispatched the Los Angeles Angels in four games, setting up an AL Championship Series showdown against the fierce rival Tampa Bay Rays.

In Game 5 of the 2008 ALCS, David's power jumpstarted an amazing Red Sox comeback. Down three games to one in the series and by a score of 7–1 in the seventh inning, David brought the Red Sox to within three runs by launching this three-run moonshot off Tampa Bay's Grant Balfour. Boston would rally to win Games 5 and 6 before falling 3–1 in Game 7. Big Papi's four hits in the series included a single, double, triple, and homer.

Frustration boiled over as Ortiz struggled to make solid contact early in the 2009 season. There was a stretch when the perennial All-Star struck out 17 times in 40 at-bats, the result, he said, of a loop in his swing caused by compensating for his wrist injury. On May 19, David was batting .203 with zero home runs, and was dropped from the third to sixth spot in the lineup. Was he washed up at age thirty-three? "People were saying, 'Oh, my God, this guy is done,'" David said.

"Rooting against Big Papi is like giving up on Santa Claus."
—Writer Bill Simmons

David finally hit his first home run of the 2009 season on May 20, sending the Fenway Faithful into a frenzy. The homer was David's first in 149 at-bats—dating back to September 22, 2008—the longest drought of his career. "My teammates said, 'What took you so long?'" David joked. "I tried it all—I was about to hit right-handed."

"Without a doubt, [Ortiz is] the premier DH in baseball. It's a hard, tough position. He's handled it unbelievably. It's tough to DH. It's a mind-set that you have to keep yourself involved in the ball game. I know that when I was a DH, my career batting average dropped, like, 20 points. It's tough. But he's figured it out."
—Frank Thomas

David circled the bases in these cleats after hitting his 270th home run as a DH to surpass the record held by Hall of Famer Frank Thomas.

David won the 2010 All-Star Game's Home Run Derby, in Anaheim, California, on July 12. The thirty-four-year-old slugger belted a total of 32 dingers at an average of 417 feet during the competition, including 11 in the final round to beat runner-up Hanley Ramirez, who hit five. When it was over, Big Papi dedicated the victory to former MLB pitcher José Lima, a fellow Dominican who died in May at age thirty-seven. Said David: "I want to dedicate this trophy and this Home Run Derby tournament to him and his family, because I know that they are going to be hurting for a long time."

For the 18th time in his career, David played the role of walk-off hero, this time swatting a three-run double in the ninth to give the Red Sox a thrilling come-from-behind 5–4 win over Detroit on July 31, 2010. The Red Sox finished the season in third place, and though David (once again) got off to a terrible start, he finished with 102 RBIs, tied with Adrián Beltré for the team lead, and 32 homers, fifth best in the league.

"He's a tremendous person, but his bat, that's what helps us win games. It's hard to imagine anyone being more important to their team than he's been to ours."
—Former Red Sox manager Terry Francona

PLAYERS HITTING 300 HOME RUNS AS A MEMBER OF THE RED SOX

Player	Year of 300th HR	Total HR with Boston
Ted Williams	1951	521
Carl Yastrzemski	1974	452
Jim Rice	1984	382
Dwight Evans	1987	379
David Ortiz	2011	445*

*through 2015 season

In April 2011, David set the major league career record for most RBIs by a designated hitter, and one month later he became the fifth player to hit 300 home runs as a member of the Red Sox. Overall, Big Papi enjoyed an excellent 2011 season, hitting .309 with 29 homers and 96 RBIs. But he melted along with his team in September, hitting just one home run in the month. Boston held a nine-game lead in the AL wild-card race, but a 7–20 September swoon cost the team a playoff spot.

"Major League Baseball is pleased to present David Ortiz with the 2011 Roberto Clemente Award. David's remarkable commitment to helping children receive essential pediatric care in the United States and the Dominican Republic makes him a wonderful choice for this honor. The legacy of the great Roberto Clemente lives on through the selfless actions of players like David and so many of his peers."
—Former MLB Commissioner Bud Selig

David received the Roberto Clemente Award prior to Game 2 of the 2011 World Series in St. Louis. Major League Baseball's ultimate recognition of community service, the Clemente Award recognizes the player who best represents the game of baseball through positive contributions, on and off the field. Ortiz's charitable work includes the David Ortiz Children's Fund, which provides medical care for children in the Dominican Republic and the United States. In 2010, the DOCF raised more than $1.5 million, providing funding for more than 200 heart operations and helping numerous children receive the care they needed.

David autographed the cap he was wearing on the day he hit career home run No. 400. He slugged 58 with Minnesota.

David belted his 400th career home run on July 4, 2012, in Oakland. Each time he crosses the plate after hitting a homer, David looks up and points both index fingers to the sky in tribute to his mother, Angela Rosa Arias, who died in a car crash in January 2002 at the age of forty-six. "My mom, she's still always there for me. Always. I think about her all the time," says David. "After my mom died, I got a big tattoo of her face on my right arm. She's still there, still watching out for me. People ask me sometimes why I point to the sky after I hit a home run, and I tell them that I'm thanking God. But I'm also thanking my mom."

"Ortiz's popularity, like his gap-toothed,
omnipresent smile,
crosses cultures and generations."
—*Sports Illustrated* writer Tom Verducci

Big Papi was enjoying a career year in 2012—or, at least, it could have been, had a strained right Achilles tendon not ended it so prematurely. Playing in just 90 games, David batted .318 with 23 homers, 60 RBIs, and 65 runs scored. But Red Sox fans would be better off simply forgetting the unmitigated disaster of the 2012 season, when Boston languished in the basement of the AL East standings.

All-Fenway Team	
LF	Ted Williams
CF	Fred Lynn
RF	Dwight Evans
3B	Wade Boggs
SS	Nomar Garciaparra
2B	Dustin Pedroia
1B	Jimmie Foxx
P	Pedro Martinez
C	Carlton Fisk
DH	David Ortiz

Fans selected David to the All-Fenway Park Team when the Red Sox commemorated Fenway Park's 100th year by honoring their greatest players prior to the 2012 regular season home finale.

INNING 8

2013: BOSTON STRONG

For his leadership in carrying the Red Sox and the resilient city of Boston to a World Series championship in 2013, David became a cultural icon in his adopted hometown. If he wasn't already, he became, in the opinion of Red Sox President Larry Lucchino, "probably the most beloved athlete in the history of Boston."

Boston Marathon Bombings

The 117th running of the Boston Marathon, the world's oldest annual marathon, was held on April 15, 2013. Around 3:00 p.m., two bombs exploded within seconds of each other near the finish line along Boylston Street, killing three spectators and wounding more than 260 people. The Red Sox players responded with heartfelt gestures in an attempt to help the city heal. It started with a team jersey hung in their dugout reading "Boston Strong" with the number 617, the city's area code. The Boston Strong logo, borrowing the Gothic "B" that adorns the team's caps, was placed on the famed Green Monster and cut into the outfield grass. But the players would not let go. "It went from a slogan to almost like a lifestyle," said outfielder Jonny Gomes. As the season progressed, the Red Sox players' ongoing response to the marathon bombings embodied the way sport can bring together a community, and it unified a World Series–bound team.

On April 20, before the first game played at Fenway Park since the Boston Marathon bombings, David addressed the crowd during a memorial service for the victims of the terrorist attack. "This jersey that we wear today, it doesn't say Red Sox, it says Boston," he told the roaring crowd before coining Boston's rallying cry. "This is our f***ing city, and no one is going to dictate our freedom. Stay strong."

David autographed this batting helmet with a special inscription: "Believe in the Red Sox Nation."

David personified the meaning of "Boston Strong" after his game-winning, three-run home run in the ninth inning beat the Texas Rangers 6–3 at Fenway Park, on June 6, 2013. It was the 12th time a Big Papi walk-off homer won a game for the Sox, the most in franchise history.

David was the 14th player to reach 2,000 career hits as a member of the Red Sox. The others are: Bobby Veach (1924), Jimmie Foxx (1938), Joe Cronin (1940), Bob Johnson (1945), Bobby Doerr (1951), Ted Williams (1955), Carl Yastrzemski (1973), Bill Buckner (1984), Jim Rice (1986), Don Baylor (1987), Dwight Evans (1988), Wade Boggs (1992), and Manny Ramirez (2006).

Ortiz received well-deserved adulation from Fenway fans on September 4, 2013, after clubbing his second home run of the game, during which he collected his 2,000th career hit. "The best thing to ever happen to me was to come to play here in Boston," David said, "because what I see every day when I get to the field is pretty much what I saw growing up. In my country, people love baseball, people live for baseball and as a player it gets you going. Our fans support this ball club better than anyone else I have seen, and getting this done, especially here at home, it was one of those things you will never forget."

Upon arrival in the batter's box, David always tucks the bat under his armpit, spits into the palm of his right batting glove, and claps his hands before digging in to face the pitcher. In 2013, the thirty-seven-year-old slugger remained one of the game's preeminent power hitters. He remained so feared that he led the majors with 27 intentional walks.

David admires his second majestic clout off Tampa Bay's David Price in Game 2 of the 2013 ALDS. This was the first time he hit two homers in a postseason game, adding to his résumé of awesomeness. Boston won the series in four games and returned to the AL Championship Series for the first time in five years.

"[David] was telling some guys before the game that he was going to hit two homers and he did. That's pretty impressive. A couple of us heard him say it, and [David Ross] and I looked at each other after he hit the second one, and I was like, 'He said he was going to do that, didn't he?' And [Ross] was like, 'He did.'"
—Former Red Sox third baseman Will Middlebrooks

David cemented his postseason legend in Game 2 of the 2013 ALCS. With the bases loaded, two outs, and Boston trailing by four runs in the eighth inning—and with the Red Sox in danger of falling into a 2–0 hole against the Tigers—David clobbered the first pitch he saw from Detroit's Joaquin Benoit over the right-field fence and into the Boston bullpen. The grand slam tied the game and keyed a dramatic comeback victory for the Red Sox, changing the face of the series and likely saving their season. "Just pandemonium," catcher David Ross described the scene in the dugout. "People going crazy. High-fiving. People screaming."

"If I tell you I was thinking about hitting a grand slam, I'd be lying to you. You try to put a good swing on the ball."
—David Ortiz

As David's grand slam cleared the fence, and the bases, Tigers right fielder Torii Hunter tumbled over the wall trying to make the catch as Boston police officer Steve Horgan raised his arms in joy. When the Red Sox won the game in the ninth inning to even the series, it felt like the Sox were destined to go all the way.

Red Sox Postseason Grand Slams			
Player	Series, Game	Pitcher, Opponent	Result
Troy O'Leary	1999 ALDS, G 5	Charles Nagy, Cleveland	W, 12–8
Johnny Damon	2004 ALCS, G 7	Javier Vazquez, Yankees	W, 10–3
J. D. Drew	2007 ALCS, G 6	Fausto Carmona, Cleveland	W, 12–2
David Ortiz	2013 ALCS, G 2	Joaquin Benoit, Detroit	W, 6–5
Shane Victorino	2013 ALCS, G 6	Jose Veras, Detroit	W, 5–2

The Cardinals fell behind early in Game 1 of the 2013 World Series, and David's two-run homer in the seventh inning finished them off, 8–1, extending the Red Sox' World Series winning streak to nine games.

Most Postseason Home Runs		
Player	HR	Plate Appearances
Manny Ramirez	29	493
Bernie Williams	22	545
Derek Jeter	20	734
Albert Pujols	19	334
Reggie Jackson	18	318
Mickey Mantle	18	273
David Ortiz	17	357
Jim Thome	17	267
Carlos Beltran	16	223
Nelson Cruz	16	167

David ripped a go-ahead two-run home run in Game 2, but those were the only Red Sox runs in a 4–2 loss. Instead of a commanding two-games-to-none lead in the series, the Sox headed to St. Louis tied with the Cards at one win apiece.

In Game 4, with the Red Sox trailing in the series two games to one, David went 3-for-3 with a double, an intentional walk, and two runs scored. He also delivered an impassioned speech to his teammates in the sixth inning, with the score 1–0, when he felt the players lacked energy. "We don't get here every day," he said. "Let's relax and play the game we know how." David's motivational words inspired the Red Sox, who responded with a three-run rally to take a lead they never surrendered. "It was like twenty-four kindergartners looking up at their teacher," said Jonny Gomes. "He got everyone's attention."

David whooped it up with teammates after the Red Sox won the 2013 World Series in six games. Behind starting pitchers Jon Lester and John Lackey, respectively, Boston won Game 5 3–1 and the finale 6–1. "Winning this World Series is special," David said after the Red Sox completed their "Boston Strong" mission. "I think it might be the most special out of all the World Series that I have been a part of."

David was all smiles at the World Series MVP Award presentation. The obvious choice for the honor, David had hit two home runs, knocked in six runs, scored seven more, batted .688, and reached base 19 times in 25 plate appearances against the Cardinals.

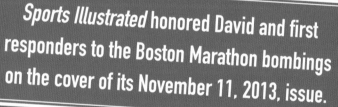
Sports Illustrated honored David and first responders to the Boston Marathon bombings on the cover of its November 11, 2013, issue.

In a touching celebratory moment, David is surrounded at the Boston Marathon finish line on Boylston Street during the Red Sox' 2013 World Series championship parade, on November 2. Big Papi and teammates placed the World Series trophy on the finish line along with a 617 "Boston Strong" Red Sox jersey to honor those affected by the bombings in a symbolic gesture that was met with cheers from the crowd. "We stick together," David said of the city. "It's a family."

David's beard was shaved for a charity supporting Boston Marathon bombing victims, during a shave-off in Boston, on November 4, 2013. The Red Sox players' beards became a symbol of their solidarity and brotherhood as they went from worst in the AL East in 2012 to first in 2013, then captured the team's third World Series title in a decade.

INNING 9

OUT WITH A BANG

The Red Sox hugely disappointed in 2014 and '15, finishing in last place both seasons, but David never relented. Defying age, Big Papi again proved to be Boston's offensive backbone, shining as the team's lone bright spot during these disappointing campaigns. He exceeded 30 homers and 100 RBIs both years, leading the team by huge margins in both categories.

David's famous presidential selfie was much re-tweeted across Red Sox Nation after Barack Obama honored the 2013 World Series champs during a ceremony at the White House on April 1, 2014.

The 2014 season began in memorable fashion, with the Red Sox receiving their 2013 World Series rings on Opening Day at Fenway Park. David, sporting his 2004 and 2007 championship rings on a chain around his neck, was handed his 2013 ring and another to honor his MVP performance. The two new rings were soon added to the necklace, creating a formidable piece of jewelry.

On August 16, 2014, David socked a pair of two-run home runs, including his 400th homer in a Red Sox uniform, and drove in six runs, to power Boston past the Houston Astros. Big Papi joined Hall of Famers Ted Williams and Carl Yastrzemski as the only players to hit 400 homers while playing with the Red Sox. According to Yastrzemski, David is the best hitter in Red Sox history, aside from Ted Williams. "As a hitter, I would say he's next to Ted," Yaz said. "I would put [Ortiz] ahead of me. He has more power than I had."

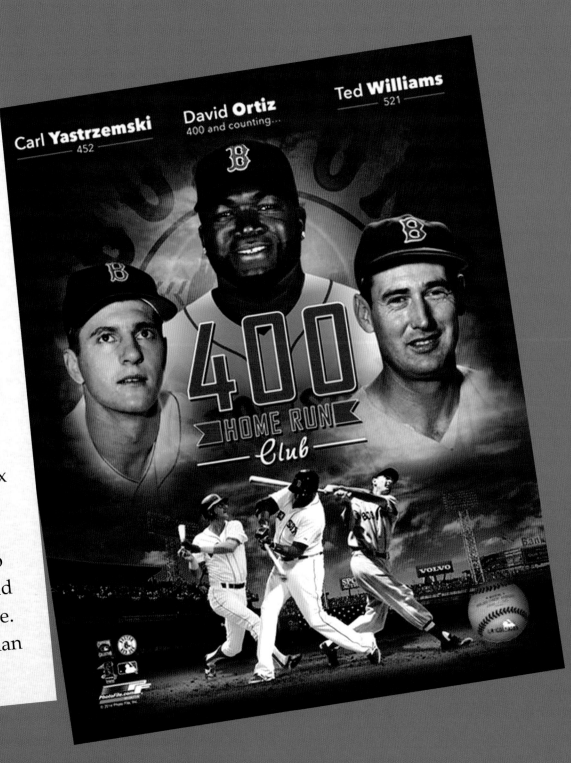

Oldest Players with 30 HRs and 100 RBIs in a Season					
Year	Age	Player	Team	HR	RBI
2015	39	David Ortiz	Red Sox	37	108
2004	39	Barry Bonds	Giants	45	101
2014	38	David Ortiz	Red Sox	35	104
2006	38	Frank Thomas	Athletics	39	114
2003	38	Rafael Palmeiro	Rangers	38	112
2002	38	Fred McGriff	Cubs	30	103
1933	38	Babe Ruth	Yankees	34	104

At age thirty-eight, David showed no signs of slowing down. His 2014 season was one of the best ever for a player his age, as he amassed 35 homers with 104 RBIs. It was his most productive season since 2007, when he was thirty-one years old.

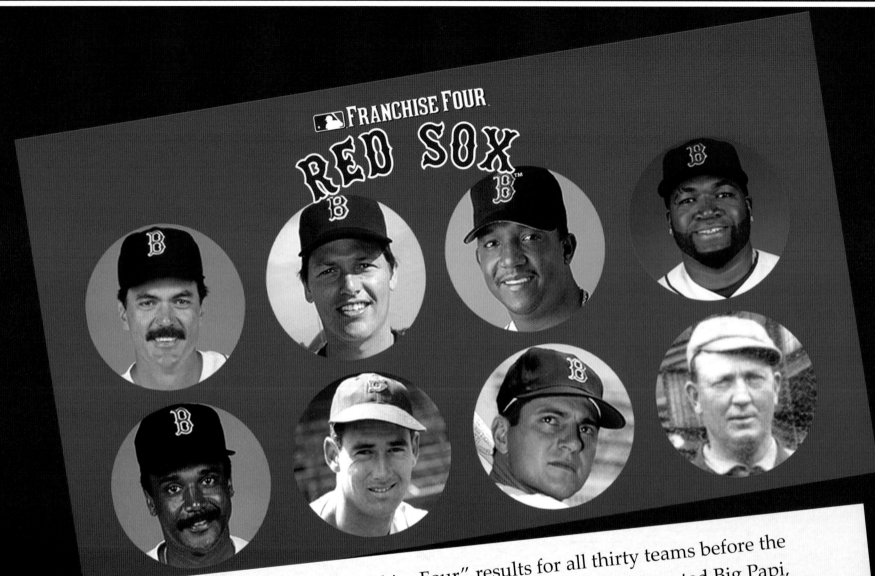

Major League Baseball released its "Franchise Four" results for all thirty teams before the 2015 All-Star Game. Drawing from over a century of Red Sox history, fans voted Big Papi, along with Ted Williams, Carl Yastrzemski, and Pedro Martinez, as the four greatest players in team history. Pictured are (top, left to right) Dwight Evans, Carlton Fisk, Martinez, Ortiz and (bottom, left to right) Jim Rice, Williams, Yaz, and Cy Young.

David watched Pedro Martinez's Hall of Fame speech and then added to his own illustrious career. Big Papi crushed two homers and drove in a career-high seven runs to propel the Red Sox to an 11–1 win over the Tigers on July 26, 2015. "Today was a day that emotions were going all over the place," said David. "I was watching the inductions. I'm not going to lie to you. It was very emotional."

David is congratulated by Jackie Bradley Jr. after becoming the 27th member of the 500-home run club, on September 12, 2015. The milestone homer was his second of the game, marking his 50th career multi–home run game. The Red Sox are the first club to have four players reach the 500-longball milestone, as Ortiz joined Jimmie Foxx (1940), Ted Williams (1960), and Manny Ramirez (2008).

Time keeps on ticking, and David keeps on slugging. In 2015, the ageless DH, still going strong, clubbed 37 home runs, the most by a Red Sox batter in nine years. It was his ninth career 30-homer season and sixth career 35-homer campaign, both of which set Red Sox records.

"David's first home run in a Red Sox uniform set the tone for the rest of his career. It was a go-ahead pinch-hit home run in the top of the 14th inning against the Angels. In that summer of 2003, David became the best slugger in all of baseball and carried the team on his back for the last three months of the season—a trend we would come to see time and again throughout his career."
—Red Sox Chairman Tom Werner

On November 18, 2015, his fortieth birthday, David announced he would retire following the 2016 season, saying, "I thought a lot about it, and for every single one of us, athletes-wise, we run out of time at some point. Life is based on different chapters, and I think I'm ready to experience the next one in my life."

EXTRA INNINGS

THE FAREWELL SEASON

As Ortiz visited rival ballparks during his 2016 good-bye tour, accepting thank-you gifts from opponents he had tormented over the years, and watching scoreboard video retrospectives documenting his many career highlights, he was worthy of every celebratory tribute earned over his 20-year thrill ride in Major League Baseball. With one final season of memories remaining, Red Sox fans hoped Big Papi's farewell season would be remembered as a victory tour.

2016 BOSTON RED SOX MEDIA GUIDE

With the acquisitions of shutdown closer Craig Kimbrel (left) and supreme starter David Price (center), the Red Sox entered 2016 as a favorite in the AL East. Of course, they would also rely on old standbys Dustin Pedroia (right) and Ortiz, who entered his final season as the 96th best player in baseball—and tops among forty-year-olds—
according to MLB Network.

David had counseled Dustin Pedroia since taking the young second baseman under his wing in the mid-2000s, and that continuous support and encouragement is evident here at their final spring training together, on March 15, 2016. Ortiz's intangible ability to play at a high level in the postseason made him the face of the modern Red Sox dynasty, but beginning in 2017, it will be Pedroia who will have to shoulder the load.

"You know what I want most of all? I would love it if the fans at Yankee Stadium gave me a standing ovation."
—Ortiz during 2016 spring training, when asked about his farewell tour.

Derek Jeter's farewell season (2014) turned into a marketing bonanza for the Yankees and Major League Baseball, and in 2016 MLB planned to cash in on Big Papi's adios campaign. Remarkably, an official "David Ortiz Final Season" logo was created, to be used on such merchandise as this T-shirt.

David takes swings in the cage during his final spring training in Fort Myers, Florida. As the sun sets on his brilliant career, it is clear that Big Papi's shadow looms as large as the other Red Sox greats: Foxx, Williams, and Yaz.

EPILOGUE

BIG PAPI'S LEGACY

Big Papi's case for Cooperstown is clear: A nine-time All-Star and a member of MLB's 500 home run club, he won six Silver Slugger Awards and finished among the top five in MVP voting five times. Yet those accolades pale in comparison to his postseason achievements: three world championship rings and two postseason series MVP awards. Soon his No. 34 will be retired and displayed atop the right field façade at Fenway, above the landing spot of so many of his greatest home runs. Among Boston's pantheon of beloved sports stars, David stands alongside Bobby Orr, Larry Bird, Bill Russell, Tom Brady, and Ted Williams.

"David's a Hall of Famer. David is as good as anyone who's ever put this uniform on. I can't imagine anybody more clutch."
—Former Red Sox pitcher Jake Peavy

The best DH in history holds hand to heart in 2013, when he became the major league record-holder for most hits by a designated hitter. David also holds the marks for most runs scored, doubles, home runs, extra-base hits, and RBIs by a DH, a position adopted by the American League in 1973.

"He's given all of our fans so much reason to cheer. I've got a lot of respect for him and the way that he's always, I think, brought a great leadership to his team. He's been a great example."
—New England Patriots quarterback Tom Brady

"It is difficult to adequately convey what David Ortiz has meant to the Boston Red Sox. For those of us who have had the honor of knowing him all these years, he has been exactly what you hope to see in a man who has been the face of this organization."
—Red Sox owner John Henry

Since his arrival in 2003, David has been the centerpiece personality of a team that has won three World Series.

References

Books

Ortiz, David, with Tony Massarotti. *Big Papi: My Story of Big Dreams and Big Hits*. New York: St. Martin's Griffin, 2008.

Shaughnessy, Dan. *The Curse of the Bambino*. New York: Penguin Books, 2004.

Periodicals and Websites

Associated Press

Atlanta Journal-Constitution

Baseball-Almanac.com

Baseball-Reference.com

Boston Globe

Boston Herald

Boston Magazine

Boston.com

David Ortiz Children's Fund

ESPN

Fox News

Knight Ridder Tribune News Service

Los Angeles Times

MLB.com

NESN

New York Times

The New Yorker

Oakland Tribune

Reuters

Seattle Times

Sports Illustrated

ThePlayersTribune.com

Toledo Blade

USA Today

WEEI

YouTube

Image credits

Chapter Openers: Authors' Collection
Page iii: AP Photo/Elise Amendola
Page 6:   AP Photo/Joe Cavaretta
Page 7:   Authors' Collection
Page 8:   AP Photo/Ed Zurga
Page 9 [left]:   AP Photo/Steve Matteo
   [right]: Authors' Collection
Page 10:   AP Photo/Tomas Van Houtryve
Page 14:   AP Photo/Elise Amendola
Page 15:   AP Photo/Elise Amendola
Page 16:   Authors' Collection
Page 17:   AP Photo/Bill Kostroun
Page 18:   AP Photo/Charles Krupa
Page 22:   AP Photo/Jeff Roberson
Page 23:   Authors' Collection
Page 24:   AP Photo/Tony Gutierrez
Page 25:   AP Photo/Winslow Townson
Page 26:   AP Photo/Amy Sancetta
Page 27:   Authors' Collection
Page 28:   AP Photo/Amy Sancetta
Page 30:   Authors' Collection
Page 31:   AP Photo/Elise Amendola
Page 32:   AP Photo/Charles
   Rex Arbogast, File
Page 33:   AP Photo/Lisa Poole
Page 34:   AP Photo/Elise Amendola

Page 38:   AP Photo/Chris O'Meara
Page 39 [left]:   AP Photo/Winslow Townson
   [right]: Authors' Collection
Page 40:   Authors' Collection
Page 41:   AP Photo/Nam Y. Huh
Page 42:   AP Photo/Mark J. Terrill
Page 43:   Authors' Collection
Page 44:   AP Photo/Frank Franklin II
Page 45:   Authors' Collection
Page 46:   AP Photo/Elise Amendola
Page 47:   AP Photo/Elise Amendola
Page 52:   AP Photo/Charles Krupa
Page 53 [left]:   AP Photo/Charles Krupa
   [right]: Authors' Collection
Page 54:   Authors' Collection
Page 55:   AP Photo/Michael Dwyer
Page 56:   AP Photo/Elise Amendola
Page 57:   AP Photo/Mark J. Terrill
Page 58:   AP Photo/Charles Krupa
Page 59:   AP Photo/Winslow Townson
Page 60:   AP Photo/Eric Gay
Page 61:   Authors' Collection
Page 62 [left]:   AP Photo/Elise Amendola
   [right]: Authors' Collection
Page 66:   Authors' Collection
Page 67:   Mark Ostow Photography